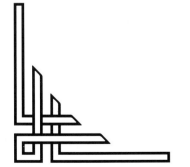

Views of

Merthyr Tydfil

and District

Volume III

Published by Merthyr Tydfil Historical Society 1994

I.S.B.N. 0 9504845 7 1

Typeset & printed by SGC Printing, Merthyr Tydfil.

FOREWORD

The Merthyr Tydfil Historical Society presents the third "Views Of Merthyr Tydfil And District", from old postcards and photographs. Over the timespan depicted we have progressed falteringly from full employment and heavy industry to a radically changed post industrial society. Where the landscape has been transformed and familiar places disappeared for ever. We hope the "views" give pleasure to all who see them.

ACKNOWLEDGEMENTS

Again we thank our friends who generously made available their post-card and photographic collections.

Mr Keith Caswell; Dr Fred Holley; Mr Leo Davies; Mr Chris Crandon; Mr Geraint James, Mrs Carolyn Jacobs, Mrs Cynthia Roberts; *(Merthyr Tydfil Library Service),* Dr E. S. Owen-Jones *(Keeper Welsh Industrial & Maritime Museum, Cardiff);* Mrs Ann Lewis; Mr Glyn Bowen; Mr Roy Beynon; Mr Kenneth J. Gunter; Mr Ceinfryn Robbins; Mrs Eira Smith; Mr Tony Mead; Mr John A. Owen; Mrs Gwen Davies; Mr Richard Francis-Williams; Mr Ron Pope.

Ron Jenkins
John A. Owen

CONTENTS

N.B. *The date with each view is only to give the reader a timescale.*

MERTHYR TYDFIL

Merthyr Tydfil High Street 1890.

Merthyr Tydfil High Street 1894.

Penydarren House 1895.

LOWER HIGH STREET, MERTHYR TYDFIL.   *Printed & Pub. by H. W. Southey & Sons, Merthyr.*

Merthyr Tydfil High Street 1903.

OLD IRON BRIDGE, MERTHYR *(Background, made at Cyfarthfa Works, 1806.*

Old & New Iron Bridges 1903.

Cyfarthfa Works Band 1905.

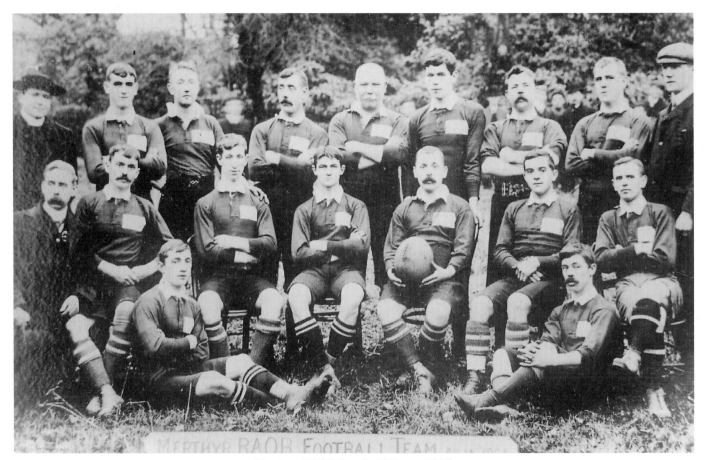

Merthyr RAOB Football Team 1905.

The County School, Merthyr-Tydfil

Merthyr Tydfil County School 1906.

9

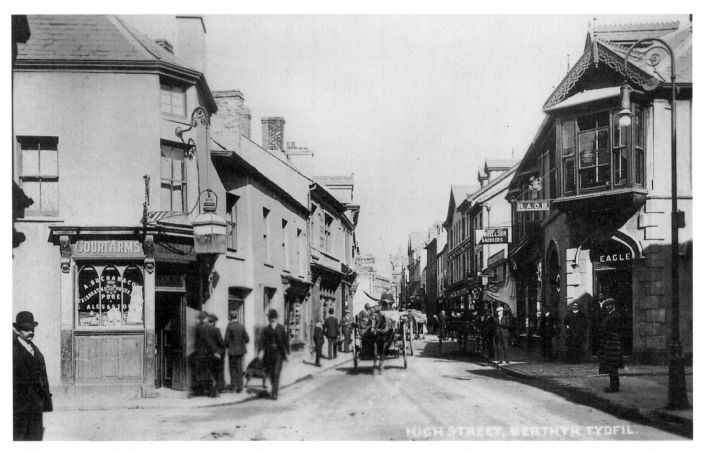

Merthyr Tydfil High Street 1907.

Merthyr Tydfil from the Angel Buildings

JV 61315

Merthyr Tydfil from the Angel Buildings 1910.

Merthyr Tydfil 1910.

Merthyr Tydfil 1910.

Merthyr Tydfil High Street 1911.

Merthyr Tydfil – The Walk 1911.

Merthyr Tydfil – Brecon Road 1911.

Merthyr Tydfil – Drum-head Service Penydarren Park 1913.

Merthyr Tydfil – Heolgerrig Colliers 1915.

Merthyr Tydfil – Clwyd-y-Fagwyr 1915.

MERTHYR TYDFIL BOROUGH POLICE.   EX-SERVICE MEN, 1914-1919.

Merthyr Tydfil Borough Police 1919.

Merthyr Tydfil, John Street 1921.

Merthyr Tydfil High Street 1921.

Merthyr Tydfil 1923.

Cymdeithas D-drama-yddol. Salem Heolgerrig.

Merthyr Tydfil – Salem Chapel Heolgerrig 1923.

Merthyr Tydfil St Mary's Catholic Church 1923.

Merthyr Tydfil High Street 1924.

Merthyr Tydfil High Street 1927.

High Street, Merthyr Tydfil.

Merthyr Tydfil High Street 1927.

High Street, Merthyr Tydfil.

Merthyr Tydfil High Street 1927.

29

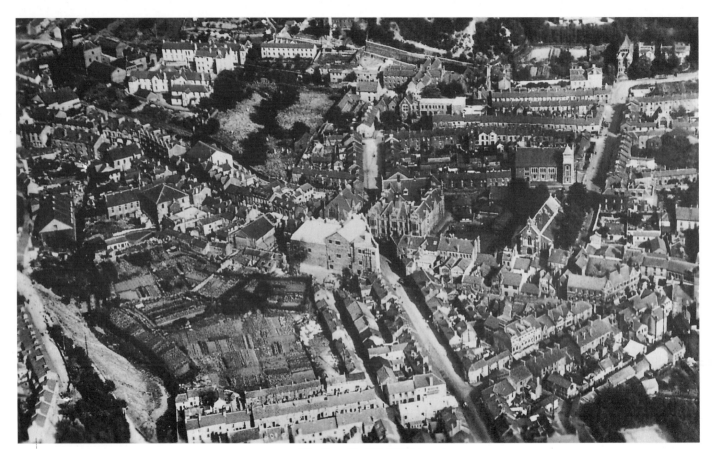

Merthyr Tydfil 1929.

Recreation Grounds, Thomastown Park, Merthyr Tydfil.

Merthyr Tydfil, Thomastown Park 1930.

Merthyr Tydfil Lower High Street 1932.

Merthyr Tydfil High Street 1932.

Merthyr Tydfil Parish Church 1938.

CARNEGIE LIBRARY, MERTHYR TYDFIL.

W.1511.

Merthyr Tydfil Carnegie Library 1938.

WATERWORKS OFFICES, MERTHYR TYDFIL.

W.1500.

Merthyr Tydfil – Castle Street 1938.

Merthyr Tydfil General Hospital 1938.

Merthyr Tydfil Cyfarthfa Castle 1938.

Merthyr Tydfil Tramcar Depot 1938.

HIGH STREET, MERTHYR TYDFIL.

Merthyr Tydfil High Street 1950.

PONTMORLAIS CIRCUS, MERTHYR TYDFIL.   W.3681.

Merthyr Tydfil High Street 1950.

Merthyr Tydfil Gwaelod-y-Garth House 1950.

Merthyr Tydfil 1961.

Merthyr Tydfil Plymouth Street 1965.

Merthyr Tydfil Bethesda Street 1970.

Merthyr Tydfil Rhydycar Cottages 1979.

Merthyr Tydfil Old Town Hall 1990.

PENYDARREN, DOWLAIS & DISTRICT

Dowlais High Street 1905.

Dowlais High Street 1905.

Dowlais Union Street 1905.

Dowlais Catholic Schools 1905.

Dowlais – Lower 1908.

Dowlais Gellyfaelog Road 1910.

Dowlais Ifor Street 1910.

Dowlais Pant 1910.

Dowlais Coal Arch 1912.

Dowlais Works – Blast Furnaces 1912.

Dowlais Works – Rolling Mills Royal Shift 1912.

Dowlais Works – Bessember Steel Plant Loco No 36, 3'-0" Gauge 1912.

Dowlais Police AFC 1912-1913.

Dowlais Christ Church Pant 1914.

Dowlais Top – Red Lion Quoits Team 1915.

Penydarren 1921.

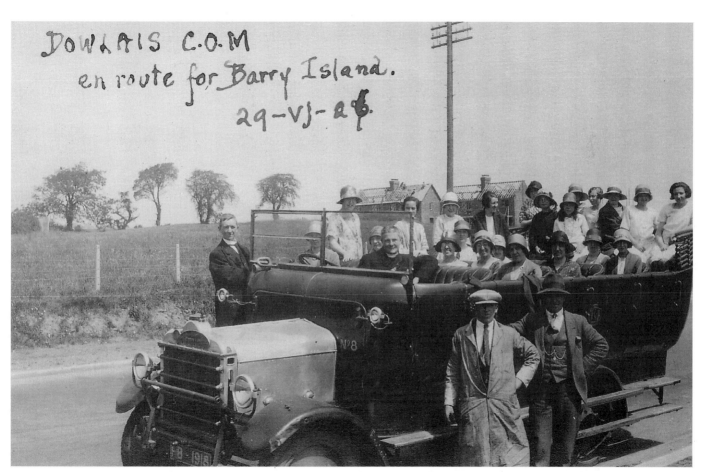

Dowlais – "Children of Mary" Outing 1926.

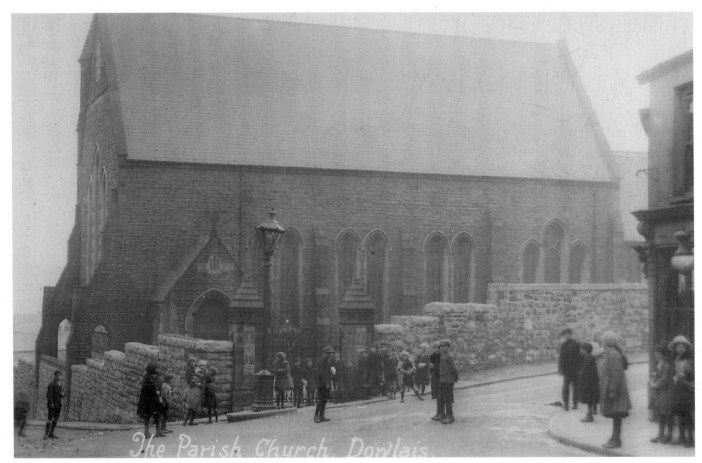

Dowlais Parish Church 1928.

Edward St., Pant, Dowlais.

Dowlais – Caeracca, Edward Street 1928.

Dowlais Central Schools 1929.

Dowlais Welfare AFC 1931-1932.

Dowlais – "Elim" Ifor Street 1937.

Dowlais Top 1953

GKB Dowlais Works AFC 1951-1952

GKB Dowlais Works Loco Gower 1953.

Dowlais ICI Loco at Pant Baths 1958.

GKN Dowlais Works – Brass Foundry 1962.

GKN Dowlais – Ingot Mould Foundry 1962.

Dowlais St Mair's Church 1963.

Dowlais St Mair's Church 1963.

GKN Dowlais Works Apprentice Foundry 1963.

Dowlais Caeharris Station 1963.

Dowlais Pant 1964.

Dowlais Pengarnddu Company Row 1968.

Dowlais High Street Old Victoria Cinema 1969.

Dowlais Ifor Street 1969.

Dowlais Central Schools 1971.

Dowlais, Caeharris Cwmcanol Street 1972.

Dowlais, Caeharris Upper Pond Street 1972.

Dowlais – Lower 1975.

Dowlais Middle 1975.

Dowlais Union Street 1975.

British Steel Dowlais Works Smiths Shop 1975.

Dowlais Parish Church 1978.

Dowlais Stables 1979.

Dowlais Ifor & Garden Streets 1980.

Dowlais Garden Street Demolition 1981.

Dowlais Ifor Street Demolition 1981.

Dowlais Stables Collapse 1982.

British Steel Dowlais Works Ingot Mould Foundry 1983.

Dowlais Penywern 1984.

Dowlais & Works 1986.

British Steel Dowlais Works – Last Slag Ladle Cast 1987.

Dowlais – Old Blast Furnace Engine House 1988.

Dowlais Stables 1993.

Dowlais Guest Memorial Hall 1993.

CEFN COED, PONTSARN, VAYNOR, PONTSTICILL

Vaynor Old & New Churches 1880s.

Pontsarn Viaduct 1903.

PONTSTICILL, TAF FECHAN, NEAR DOWLAIS.

Cartwright, Printers & Publishers,
Dowlais.

Pontsticill 1904.

Cefn Coed High Street 1912.

Pontsarn Viaduct 1912.

VAYNOR COTTAGE PONTSARN H. 3. 12. 4.

Vaynor 1916.

Pontsarn Sanatorium 1916.

The Viaduct, Cefn. 2549

Cefn Viaduct 1921.

St John's Church Cefn Coed 1923.

Cefn Coed Bridge 1924.

Pontsticill Waterworks 1927.

"Taf Fechan" Road & Reservoir, Pontsticill.

Pontsticill Reservoir 1928.

Cefn Coed 1929.

Lower High Street, with War Memorial, Cefn Coed.

Cefn Coed High Street 1937.

Cefn Coed High Street 1938.

ABERCANAID, PENTREBACH, TROEDYRHIW, ABERFAN, MERTHYR VALE, QUAKERS' YARD, TREHARRIS, BEDLINOG

Bedlinog 1900.

Merthyr Vale, Rhymney Railway Viaduct

Merthyr Vale 1903.

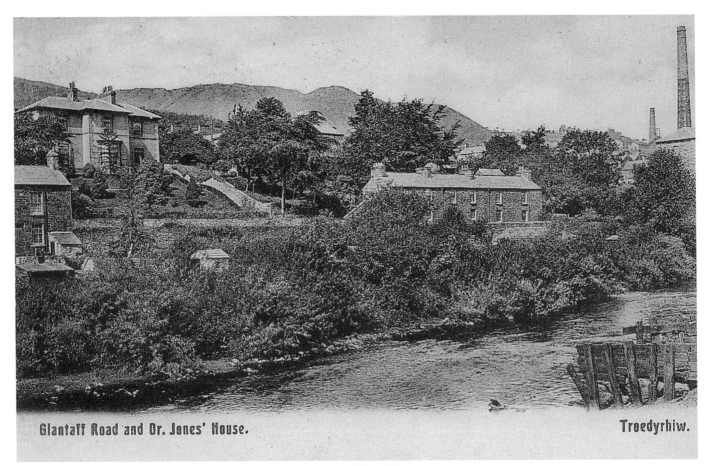

Glantaff Road and Dr. Jones' House.

Troedyrhiw.

Troedyrhiw 1904.

St. Peters Church.

Abercanaid.

Abercanaid – St Peter's Church 1904.

125

Bedlinog Inn 1906

Treharris AFC 1905-1906.

Aberfan 1907.

Merthyr Vale Colliery 1908.

Quakers' Yard – Thomas & Evans Delivery 1909.

GKN Bedlinog Colliery 1910.

Bedlinog Nantwen Colliery No2 Rescue Brigade 1910.

Quakers' Yard Truants School 1910.

Treharris – The Park 1912.

Troedyrhiw Boys Brigade 1912.

Quakers' Yard Tornado 1913.

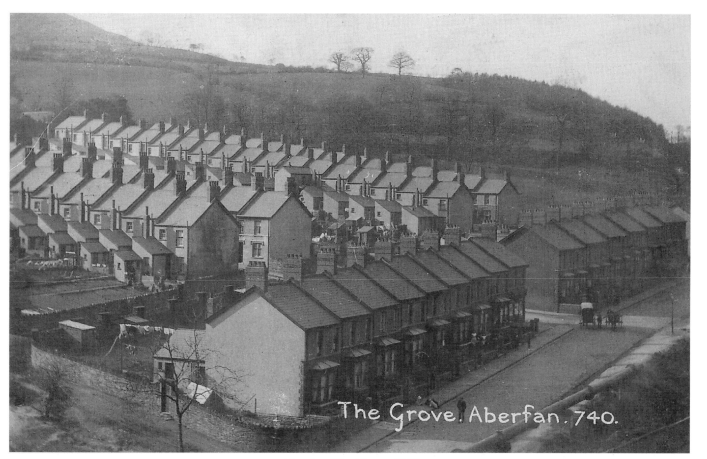

Aberfan The Grove 1915.

Merthyr Vale Colliery 1915.

Aberfan 1915.

Aberfan 1916.

4157. Fox Street № 2. Treharris. Ernest. T. Bush

Treharris Fox Street 1920.

Treharris Colliery 1925.

Aberfan 1929.

Pentrebach Social Centre AFC 1931.

Bedlinog Co-operative Society 1932.

The Square, (2) Bedlinog. (from the Mountain) 853

Bedlinog – The Square 1937.

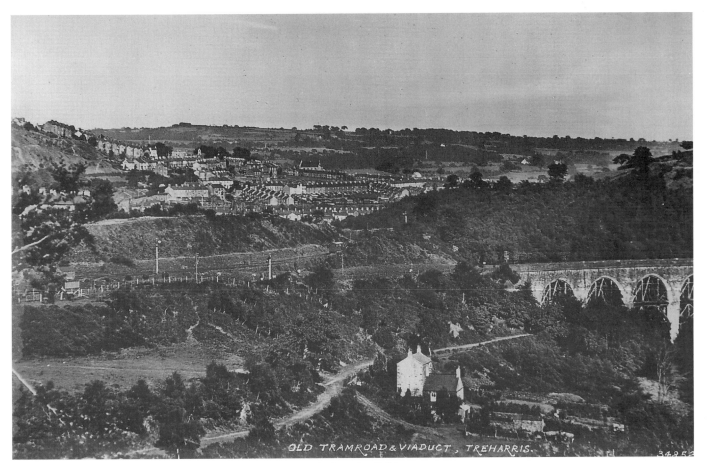

Treharris 1937.

Treharris – Cilhaul 1938.

Aberfan 1948.

Pentrebach – Site of Dyffryn Ironworks & Colliery 1961.

Troedyrhiw Dynevor Arms 1972.

Abercanaid Llwynyreos Inn 1972.

Pentrebach Triangle Houses & Long Row 1972.